By Lambertus Oosthuizen

Published by Marc Schindler Publishing
ISBN PAPERBACK: 9798569150335
Cover design by Marc Schindler

Foreword

Quotes have always fascinated me. They are little insights into life. Whether we are expiring something positive, negative, frightening or inspiring, quotes often gives us a succinct and unique point of view to what I am experiencing. And who does not want to be guided by the insights of the greatest minds ?

But it is more than just a few words spoken by a famous person. Inspirational or motivational quotes capture and appeal our subconscious mind, creativity is found subtly embedded there. Inspirational quotes may instantaneously change our entire thought process, directing our energies towards a positive path. It is clear that when the subconscious is constantly filled with a flow of positive commands, there is uplift in our general outlook and personality.

For my wife, whom I hope to annoy for many years to come.

Table of Contents

Renewal

1

Change is supremely inconvenient, uncomfortable and
naturally scary. Yet we only move through life through
the process of change, reinvention and renewal, and so
bravery is our quintessential rebel for pushing us past
our own limiting beliefs and behaviours. Bravery is
feeling the fear, immersing yourself into it and through
it so you can come out the other side.

Christine Evangelou

2

When we work with love we renew the spirit; that
renewal is an act of self-love, it nurtures our growth.

Bell Hooks

3

Rest when you're
weary. Refresh and renew
yourself, your body, your
mind, your spirit. Then get
back to work.

Ralph Marston

4

Genius is the ability to renew one's emotions in daily experience.

Paul Cezanne

5

The dry seasons in life do not last. The spring rains will come again.

Sarah Ban Breathnach

6

We must always change, renew, rejuvenate ourselves; otherwise, we harden.

Johann Wolfgang von Goethe

7

What's so fascinating and frustrating and great about life is that you're constantly starting over, all the time, and I love that.

Billy Crystal

8

One should count each day a separate life.

Seneca

9

Take the first step in faith. You don't have to see the whole staircase, just take the first step.

Martin Luther King, Jr.

10

It's humbling to start fresh. It takes a lot of courage. But it can be reinvigorating. You just have to put your ego on a shelf & tell it to be quiet.

Jennifer Ritchie Payette

11

Celebrate endings, for they precede new beginnings.

Jonathan Lockwood Huie

12

If you don't like the road you're walking, start paving another one.

Dolly Parton

13

If I must start somewhere, right here and now is the best place imaginable.

Richelle E. Goodrich

14

Recreate your life, always, always. Remove the stones, plant rose bushes and make sweets. Begin again.

Cora Coralina

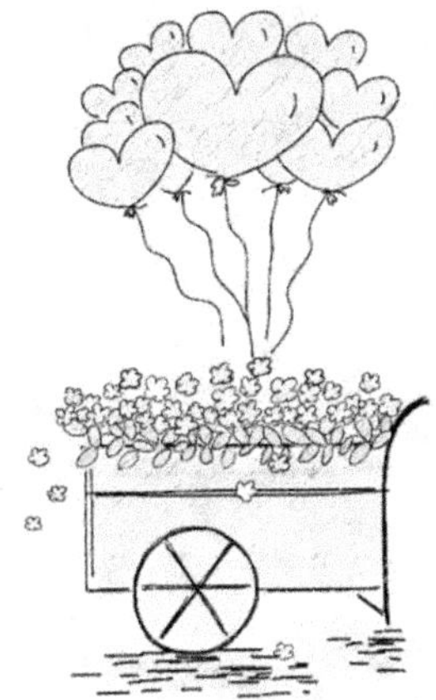

15

If all you can do is crawl, start crawling.

Rumi

16

Every day is a new beginning. Treat it that way. Stay away from what might have been, and look at what can be.

Marsha Petrie Sue

17

The secret to change is to focus all of your energy, not
on fighting the old, but on building the new.

Socrates

18

Every single cell in the human body replaces itself over
a period of seven years. That means there's not even the
smallest part of you now that was part of you seven
years ago.

Steven Hall

19

If you are renewed by grace, and
were to meet your old self, I am
sure you would be very anxious to
get out of his company.

Charles H. Spurgeon

20

Renewal requires opening yourself up to new ways of
thinking and feeling.

Deborah Day

21

True, it's not over till it's over. And
even when it's over, it just begins
again.

Kate McGahan

22

When we work with love we renew the spirit; that
renewal is an act of self-love, it nurtures our growth.

Bell Hooks

23

There is no such thing as completion. These are only
stages in an endless progression. There are no final
outcomes or decisions, since nothing ever stays the
same.

Frederick Lenz

24

You are never too old to set another
goal or to dream a new dream.

C.S. Lewis

25

You must learn a new way to think
before you can master a new way to be.

Marianne Williamson

26

So long as a person is capable of self-renewal they are a
living being.

Henri Frederic Amiel

Recovery is an important
word and a vital concept. It
means renewal of life and
energy. Knowing how and
when to recover may prove
to be the most important
skill in your life.

James E. Loehr

28

If you want a new tomorrow,
then make new choices
today.

Tim Fargo

29

I can hardly wait for tomorrow, it means a new life for
me each and every day.

Stanley Kunitz

30

If you want to fly, you have to give up what weighs you
down.

Roy T. Bennett

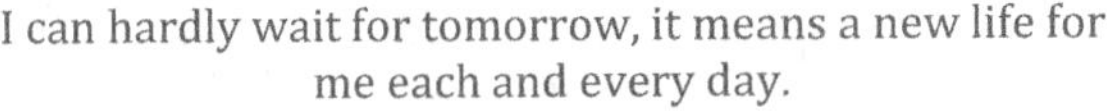

Family

31

The informality of family life
is a blessed condition that
allows us all to become our
best while looking our worst.

Marge Kennedy

32

In time of test, family is best.

Burmese Proverb

33

Rejoice with your family in the beautiful land of life.

Albert Einstein

34

When all the dust is settled and all the crowds are gone,
the things that matter are faith, family, and friends.

Barbara Bush

35

Everyone needs a house to live in, but a supportive
family is what builds a home.

Anthony Liccione

36

The bond that links your true family is not
one of blood, but of respect and joy in each
other's life.

Richard Bach

37

Family is a life jacket in the stormy sea of life.

J.K. Rowling

38

Family means no one gets left behind or forgotten.

George Bernard Shaw

39

Of course we go through tough times. When we go
through tough times we work through it as a unit, as a
family.

David Beckham

40

The family is link to our past, bridge to our future.

Alex Haley

41

Family is not an important thing. It's everything.

Michael J. Fox

42

A happy family is but an earlier heaven.

George Bernard Shaw

43

The other night I ate at a real nice family restaurant. Every table had an argument going.

George Carlin

44

Each ingredient enhances the others; each batch has its own characteristics; and it needs time to simmer to reach full flavor.

Marge Kennedy

45

The family, that dear octopus from whose tentacles we
never quite escape, nor in our innermost hearts never
quite wish to.

Dodie Smith

46

You go through life wondering
what is it all about but at the
end of the day it's all about
family.

Rod Stewart

47

Nothing else matters so much as long as you can come
home and be with your family.

Patrick Dempsey

48

You don't choose your family. They are God's gift to you,
as you are to them.

Desmond Tutu

49

Families are
like fudge -
mostly sweet,
with a few
nuts.

Les Dawson

50

I think the older you get, the more you realize how
important life is, the more you think about your family.

Wes Welker

51

If you cannot get rid of the family skeleton, you may as
well make it dance.

George Bernard Shaw

52

My perfect weekend is going for
a walk with my family in the
park. I don't think there's
anything better.

Anne Wojcicki

53

The only rock I know that stays steady, the
only institution I know that works, is the family.

Lee Iacocca

54

Family first, always, no matter what the situation.

Baker Mayfield

55

Family is my fun.

Brad Garlinghouse

56

The family is one of
nature's masterpieces.

George Santayana

57

In family life, love is the
oil that eases friction,
the cement that binds
closer together, and the
music that brings
harmony.

Friedrich Nietzsche

58

It didn't matter how big our house was; it mattered that there was love in it.

Peter Buffett

59

Call it a clan, call it a network, call it a tribe, call it a family: Whatever you call it, whoever you are, you need one.

Jane Howard

60

A dysfunctional family is any family with more than one person in it.

Mary Karr

Friends

61

True friends are always together in spirit.

L.M. Montgomery

62

If you live to be 100, I hope I live to be
100 minus 1 day, so I never have to live
without you.

Winnie the Pooh

63

True friendship comes when the silence between two
people is comfortable.

David Tyson

64

A friend is someone who
understands your past, believes in
your future, and accepts you just the
way you are.

Unknown

65

The real test of friendship is can you
literally do nothing with the other person? Can you
enjoy those moments of life that are utterly simple?

Eugene Kennedy

66

It is not a lack of love, but a lack of friendship that
makes unhappy marriages.

Friedrich Nietzsche

Friendship is the hardest thing in the world to explain. It's not something you learn in school. But if you haven't learned the meaning of friendship, you really haven't learned anything.

Muhammad Ali

68

If you go looking for a friend, you're going to find
they're very scarce. If you go out to be a friend, you'll
find them everywhere.

Zig Ziglar

69

Friendship is the only cement that will
ever hold the world together.

Woodrow T. Wilson

70

Life is an awful, ugly place to not have a best friend.

Sarah Dessen

71

Friends are those rare people who ask
how we are and then wait to hear the
answer.

Ed Cunningham

A true friend is someone who thinks that you are a good egg even though he knows that you are slightly cracked.

Bernard Meltzer

73

There is nothing better than a friend, unless it is a friend with chocolate.

Linda Grayson

It is not so much our friends' help that helps us, as the confidence of their help.

Epicurus

75

Do I not destroy my enemies when I make them my friends?

Abraham Lincoln

76

If it's very painful for you to criticize your friends — you're safe in doing it. But if you take the slightest pleasure in it, that's the time to hold your tongue.

Alice Duer Miller

77

Truly great friends are hard to find, difficult to leave, and impossible to forget.

Unknown

78

No friendship is an accident.

O. Henry

79

Friends are the family you choose.

Jess C. Scott

80

It's the friends you can call up at 4
a.m. that matter.

Marlene Dietrich

81

Friendship is so weird...you just pick a human you've
met and you're like 'Yep, I like this one' and you just do
stuff with them.

Unknown

82

In everyone's life, at some time, our inner fire goes out.
It is then burst into flame by an encounter with another
human being. We should all be thankful for those people
who rekindle the inner spirit.

Albert Schweitzer

Experts on romance say for a happy marriage there has
to be more than a passionate love. For a lasting union,
they insist, there must be a genuine liking for each
other. Which, in my book, is a good definition for
friendship.

Marilyn Monroe

84

A good friend is like a four-leaf clover; hard to find and
lucky to have.   *Irish
Proverb*

85

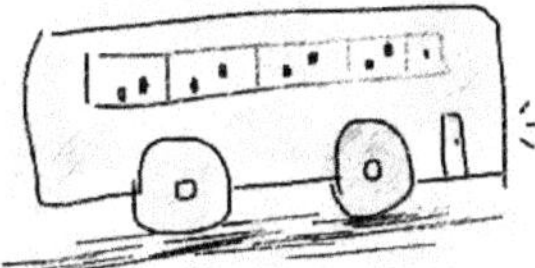

Lots of people want to
ride with you in the limo,
but what you want is
someone who will take
the bus with you when
the limo breaks down.

Oprah Winfrey

86

To the world you may be just
one person, but to one person
you may be the world.

Dr. Seuss

87

A real friend is one who walks
in when the rest of the world
walks out.

Walter Winchell

88

A friend who understands your tears is much more
valuable than a lot of friends who only know your smile.

Unknown

89

Sitting silently beside a friend who is hurting may be the best gift we can give.

Unknown

90

A good friend is a connection to life — a tie to the past, a road to the future, the key to sanity in a totally insane world.

Lois Wyse

91

Friendships are considered to exist when pleasure is taken in the company of another; when being with someone becomes a duty, rather than a preference, friendships begin to wane.

Psychology Today

92

Life is partly what we make it, and partly what it is made by the friends we choose.

Tennessee Williams

Perseverance

93

You learn from every mistake you make, so therefore –
ram on!

Tom Hanks

94

As we fall down we've got to get up and get going again,
he says. That's what life's all about. Everyone has their
setbacks and times when they fell.

Arnold Schwarzenegger

95

I have faith 51% of the time, and that turns the tide just
enough.

Tom Hanks

96

Fall seven times and stand up eight.

Japanese Proverb

97

It's not that I'm so smart, it's just that I stay with problems longer.

Albert Einstein

98

Failure is only the opportunity to begin again, this time more intelligently.

Henry Ford

99

Success is the sum of small efforts, repeated day in and day out.

Robert Collier

100

Perseverance is the hard work you do after you get tired of doing the hard work you already did.

Newt Gingrich

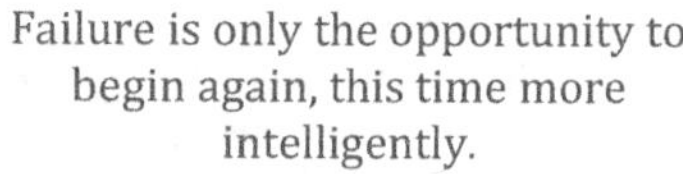

101

We will either find a way or
make one.

Hannibal

102

It always seems impossible until
it's done.

Nelson Mandela

103

The best way out is always through.

Robert Frost

104

A winner is just a loser who tried one more time.

George M. Moore Jr.

105

The man who moves a mountain begins by carrying
away small stones.

Confucius

106

I am a slow walker, but I never walk
back.

Abraham Lincoln

107

Every strike brings me closer to the next
home run.

Babe Ruth

108

Courage is not having the strength to go on; it is going
on when you don't have the strength.

Theodore Roosevelt

109

Perseverance, secret of all triumphs.

Victor Hugo

110

Success is no accident. It is hard work, perseverance,
learning, studying, sacrifice and most of all, love of what
you are doing or learning to do.

Pele

111

Never, never, never, never
give up.

Winston Churchill

112

Just remember, you can do anything you set your mind
to, but it takes action, perseverance, and facing your
fears.

Gillian Anderson

113

The will to persevere is often the difference between
failure and success.

David Sarnoff

114

He conquers who endures.

Persius

115

Energy and persistence conquer all
things.

Benjamin Franklin

There are only two mistakes one can make along the road to truth; not going all the way, and not starting.

Buddha

Let me tell you the secret that has led to my goal. My strength lies solely in my tenacity.

Louis Pasteur

It does not matter how slowly you go so long as you do not stop.

Confucius

119

You may have to fight a battle more than once to win it.

Margaret Thatcher

120

Through perseverance many people win success out of
what seemed destined to be certain failure.

Benjamin Disraeli

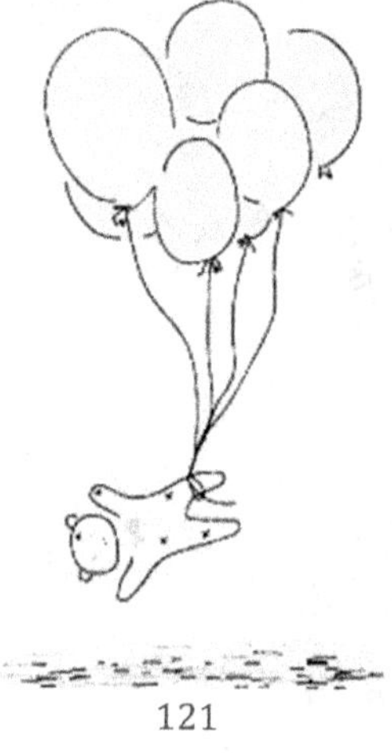

121

Just because you fail once doesn't mean you're gonna
fail at everything.

Marilyn Monroe

122

Purity, patience and perseverance are the three
essentials to success and above all love.

Swami Vivekananda

123

Continuous effort–not strength or intelligence–is the
key to unlocking our potential.

Winston Churchill

Gratitude

124

Appreciation is a wonderful thing. It makes what is excellent in others belong to us as well.

Voltaire

125

Learn to be thankful for what you already have, while you pursue all that you want.

Jim Roh

126

'Thank you' is the best prayer that anyone could say. I say that one a lot. Thank you expresses extreme gratitude, humility, understanding.

Alice Walker

*Enjoy the little things, for one day
you may look back and realize they
were the big things.*

Robert Brault

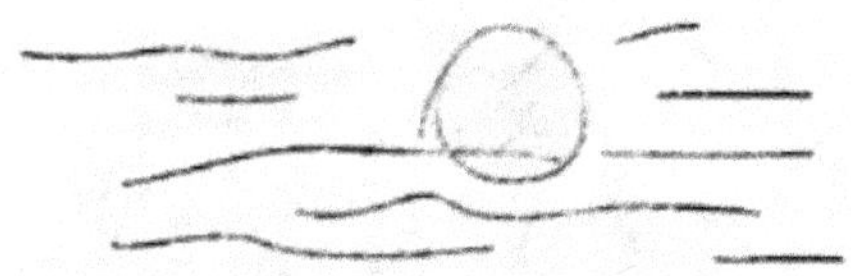

128

My socks may not match, but my feet are
always warm

Maureen McCullough

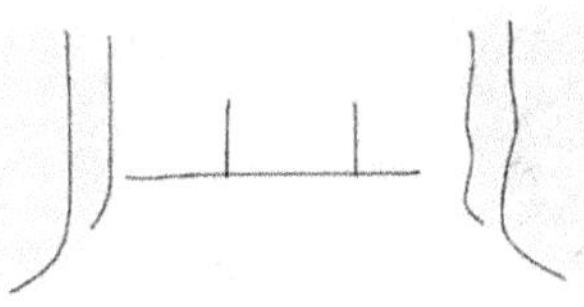

129

When I started counting my
blessings, my whole life turned
around.

Willie Nelson

130

Gratitude is a quality similar to electricity: It must be
produced and discharged and used up in order to exist
at all.

William Faulkner

131

Some people grumble that
roses have thorns; I am grateful
that thorns have roses.

Alphonse Karr

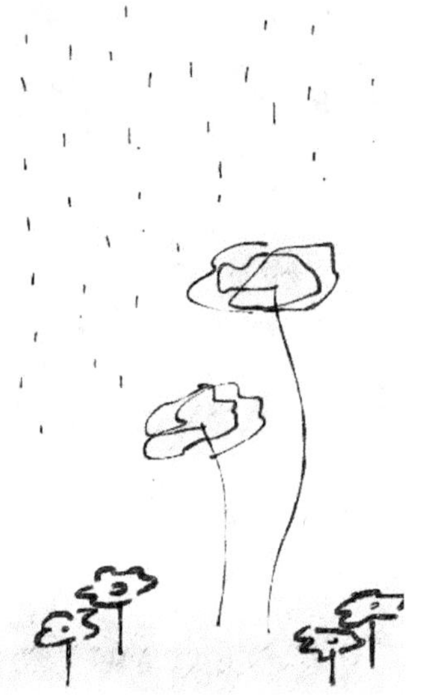

132

A thankful heart is not only the
greatest virtue, but the parent
of all the other virtues.

Cicero

133

This a wonderful day. I've never seen this one before.

Maya Angelou

134

Enough is a feast.

Buddhist Proverb

135

As we express our gratitude, we must never forget that
the highest appreciation is not to utter words but to live
by them.

John F. Kennedy

136

The way to develop the best that is in a person is by
appreciation and encouragement.

Charles Schwab

137

Stop now. Enjoy the moment. It's now or never.

Maxime Lagacé

138

Gratitude is riches. Complaint is poverty.

Doris Day

139

Gratitude is the healthiest of all human emotions. The more you express gratitude for what you have, the more likely you will have even more to express gratitude for.

Zig Ziglar

140

When you view your world with an attitude of gratitude, you are training yourself to focus on the good in life.

Paul J. Meyer

141

Of all the characteristics needed for both a happy and
morally decent life, none surpasses gratitude. Grateful
people are happier, and grateful people are more
morally decent.

Dennis Prager

142

When we give cheerfully and accept gratefully,
everyone is blessed.

Maya Angelou

143

The trick is to be grateful when your
mood is high and graceful when it is
low.

Richard Carlson

144

Be grateful for what you have and stop complaining – it
bores everybody else, does you no good, and doesn't
solve any problems.

Zig Ziglar

145

The root of joy is gratefulness.

David Steindl-Rast

146

If you do not appreciate every day of your life, who said
that the days and years will be an asset for the future?

Sunday Adelaja

147

Most people are unhappy because they're focused on
what they want rather than appreciating what they
have.

Marty Rubin

148

You won't be happy with more until you're happy with what you've got.

Viki King

149

Joy is the simplest form of gratitude.

Karl Barth

150

Gratitude will shift you to a higher frequency, and you
will attract much better things.

Rhonda Byrne

151

Gratitude is when
memory is stored in the
heart and not in the
mind.

Lionel Hampton

152

Be thankful for what you have;
you'll end up having more. If
you concentrate on what you
don't have, you will never, ever
have enough.

Oprah Winfrey

153

When it comes to life the
critical thing is whether you
take things for granted or take them with gratitude.

G.K. Chesterton

154

Gratitude unlocks the fullness of life. It turns what we
have into enough, and more.

Melody Beattie

155

If a fellow isn't thankful for
what he's got, he isn't likely to
be thankful for what he's going
to get.

Frank A. Clark

156

Gratitude is what you feel when
you want what you already
have.

James Clear

157

Optimism is really rooted in gratitude,"
said Fox. "Optimism is sustainable when you keep
coming back to gratitude.

Michael J. Fox

158

We must find time to stop and thank the people who
make a difference in our lives.

John F. Kennedy

159

I was complaining that I had no shoes till I met a man
who had no feet.

Confucius

160

Our favorite attitude should be gratitude.

Zig Ziglar

161

Entitlement is such a cancer,
because it is void of
gratitude.

Adam Smith

162

There are always flowers for
those who want to see them.

Henri Matisse

163

Expressing gratitude is a natural state of being and
reminds us that we are all connected.

Valerie Elster

164

You don't get blessed, and feel blessed. You have to first
feel blessed, then the blessings come to you.

Roman Price

165

The thankful receiver bears a plentiful harvest.

William Blake

Be Yourself

166

Why compare yourself with others? No one in the entire world can do a better job of being you than you.

Unknown

167

Everybody wants to be somebody; nobody wants to grow.

Johann Wolfgang von Goethe

168

We only become what we are by the radical and deep-seated refusal of that which others have made of us.

Jean-Paul Sartre

169

I am somebody. I am me. I like being me. And I need nobody to make me somebody.

Louis L'Amour

170

It doesn't matter who you've been.
Now, it is about who you are willing
to be.

Sheldon Ginsberg

171

The best way to find yourself is to
lose yourself in the service of
others.

Mahatma Gandhi

172

Don't lose your real self in the search for acceptance by
others.

Lora A.R.

173

Never be bullied into silence. Never allow yourself to be
made a victim. Accept no one's definition of your life;
define yourself.

Harvey Fierstein

174

Unless you change how you are, you will always have what you've got.

Jim Rohn

175

To be beautiful means to be yourself. You don't need to be accepted by others. You need to accept yourself.

Thich Nhat Hanh

176

Don't change so someone will like you. Be yourself and the right people will like and love the real you.

Mastin Kipp

177

You can't let other people tell you who you are.. You have to decide that for yourself .

Robert Kiyosaki

178

Conquer yourself and the world lies at your feet.

St. Augustine

179

Be who you are and say what you feel because those who mind don't matter and those who matter don't mind.

Dr. Seuss

180

The greatest thing in the world is to know how to belong to oneself.

Alexa Vega

181

I would rather be a little nobody, than to be an evil somebody.

Abraham Lincoln

182

Follow your inner moonlight; don't
hide the madness.

Allen Ginsberg

183

If you end up with a boring
miserable life because you listened
to your mom, your dad, your
teacher, your priest, or some guy on
television telling you how to do your
shit, then you deserve it.

Frank Zappa

184

Imperfection is beauty, madness is genius, and it's
better to be absolutely ridiculous than absolutely
boring.

Marilyn Monroe

185

Never dull your shine for somebody else.

Tyra Banks

186

I think everybody's weird. We should all celebrate our individuality and not be embarrassed or ashamed of it.

Johnny Depp

187

Kites rise high against the wind, not with it.

Winston Churchill

188

A girl should be two things:
who and what she wants.

Coco Chanel

189

Wanting to be someone else is a waste of who you are.

Kurt Cobain

190

When you dance to your own rhythm,
life taps its toes to your beat.

Terri Guillemets

191

I'm the one that's got to die
when it's time for me to
die, so let me live my life the way I
want to.

Jimi Hendrix

192

It's just better to be yourself than to try to be some
version of what you think the other person wants.

Matt Damon

193

Don't compromise yourself – you're all you have.

John Grisham

194

When you are content to be simply yourself and don't compare or compete, everyone will respect you.

Lao Tzu

195

To shine your brightest light is to be who you truly are.

Roy T. Bennett

196

Don't worry what people say or what people think. Be yourself.

Brett Hull

Be Brave

197

Do one thing every day that scares you.

Eleanor Roosevelt

198

Have the courage to follow your
heart and intuition. They somehow
already know what you truly want
to become.

Steve Jobs

199

What does it mean if I'm afraid? Does it mean something
bad is going to happen? No, It doesn't mean something
bad is going to happen. It just means that you have the
chance to be brave.

C. JoyBell C

200

Even if your size is microscopic, and still the heart is brave. You are the man.

C. Jay

201

Find out what you're afraid of and go live there.

Chuck Palahniuk

202

You can't be brave if you've only had wonderful things happen to you.

Mary Tyler Moore

203

I cannot teach you violence, as I do not myself believe in it. I can only teach you not to bow your heads before any one even at the cost of your life.

Mahatma Gandhi

204

Fear can keep a man out of danger but courage only can support him in it.

Thomas Fuller

205

Be brave. Take risks. Nothing can substitute experience.

Paulo Coelho

206

You can choose courage, or you can choose comfort, but you cannot choose both.

Brené Brown

207

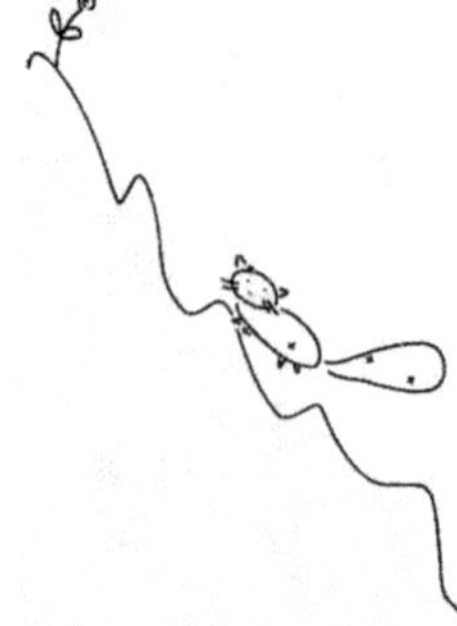

The brave don't live forever but the cautious don't live at all. The only thing that's truly terrifying is the unlived life.

Bill See

208

I learned that courage was not the
absence of fear, but the triumph over it.
The brave man is not he who does not
feel afraid, but he who conquers that
fear.

Nelson Mandela

209

A hero is no braver than an ordinary man, but he is
brave five minutes longer.

Ralph Waldo Emerso

210

Forgiveness is a virtue of the brave.

Indira Gandhi

211

When a brave man takes a stand, the spines of others
are often stiffened.

Billy Graham

212

You cannot swim for new horizons until you have courage to lose sight of the shore.

William Faulkner

213

So long as we are brave enough to accept the consequences of our actions, no one can take away our freedom of choice.

Mike Norton

214

The best way out is always through.

Robert Frost

215

Moral excellence comes about as a result of habit. We become just by doing just acts, temperate by doing temperate acts, brave by doing brave acts.

Aristotle

216

Fortune always favors the brave, and never helps a man
who does not help himself.

P. T. Barnum

217

Let us all be brave enough to die the death of a martyr,
but let no one lust for martyrdom.

Mahatma Gandhi

218

Courage is being scared to
death and saddling up anyway.

John Wayne

219

He who is brave is free.

Seneca

220

Courage is contagious. When a brave man takes a stand,
the spines of others are often stiffened

Billy Graham

221

It takes courage to grow up and
become who you really are.

E.E. Cummings

222

The real man smiles in trouble, gathers strength from
distress, and grows brave by reflection.

Thomas Paine

223

Take chances, make mistakes. That's how you grow.
Pain nourishes your courage. You have to fail in order to
practice being brave.

Mary Tyler Moore

224

I can't pretend that I'm brave and that I can beat the
whole world.

Nelson Mandela

225

Life shrinks or expands in proportion to one's courage.

Anais Nin

Experience

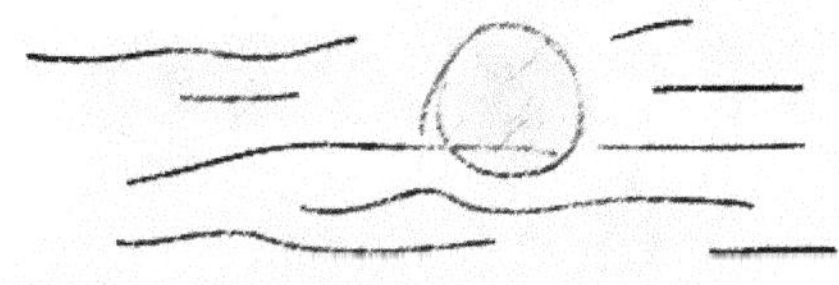

226

Never regret. If it's good, it's wonderful. If it's bad, it's experience.

Victoria Holt

227

Experience is the teacher of all things.

Julius Caesar

228

Nothing is a waste of time if you use the experience wisely.

Auguste Rodin

229

"Experiences are savings which a miser puts aside.

Karl Kraus

230

Experience: that most brutal of teachers. But you learn, my God do you learn.

C.S. Lewis

231

Strength does not come from winning. Your struggles develop your strengths. When you go through hardships and decide not to surrender, that is strength.

Arnold Schwarzenegger

232

Experience is that marvellous thing that enables you to recognize a mistake when you make it again.

Franklin P. Jones

You gain strength, courage and confidence by every experience in which you really stop to look fear in the face.

Eleanor Roosevelt

234

Experience is a safe light to walk by, and he is not a rash man who expects to succeed in future from the same means which have secured it in times past.

Wendell Phillips

235

We can teach from our experience, but we cannot teach experience.

Sasha Azevedo

236

Experience is the name everyone gives to their mistakes.

Oscar Wilde

237

Experience is a good school. But the fees are high.

Heinrich Heine

238

God will not look you over for medals degrees or diplomas, but for scars.

Elbert Hubbard

239

Good judgment comes from experience, and experience comes from bad judgment.

Unknown

240

One thorn of experience is worth a whole wilderness of warning.

James Russell Lowell

241

Experience is what you get while looking for something else.

Federico Fellini

242

The only source of knowledge is experience.

Albert Einstein

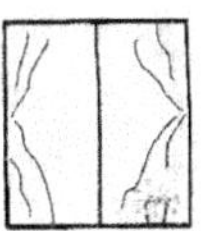

243

Do you know the difference between
education and experience? Education is
when you read the fine print; experience
is what you get when you don't.

Pete Seeger

244

Experience makes more timid men than it does wise
ones.

Josh Billings

245

There is only one thing more painful than learning from
experience, and that is not learning from experience.

Laurence J. Peter

246

Experience: that most brutal of teachers. But you learn,
my God do you learn.

C.S. Lewis

247

Human beings, who are almost unique in having the
ability to learn from the experience of others, are also
remarkable for their apparent disinclination to do so.

Douglas Adams

248

Years teach us more than books.

Berthold Auerbach

249

There's a beauty to wisdom and
experience that cannot be faked. It's
impossible to be mature without
having lived.

Amy Grant

250

Wisdom comes from experience. Experience is
often a result of lack of wisdom.

Terry Pratchett

251

We are not human beings having a spiritual experience.
We are spiritual beings having a human experience.

Pierre Teilhard De Chardin

252

Experience is one thing you can't get for nothing.

Oscar Wilde

Be Humble

253

Sense shines with a double lustre when it is set in humility. An able yet humble man is a jewel worth a kingdom.

William Penn

254

Talent is God given. Be humble. Fame is man-given. Be grateful. Conceit is self-given. Be careful.

John Wooden

255

The biggest challenge after success is shutting up about it.

Criss Jami

256

To be humble to superiors is duty, to equals courtesy, to inferiors nobleness.

Benjamin Franklin

257

The praise that comes from love does not make us vain,
but more humble.

James M. Barrie

258

A person can
achieve
everything by
being simple and
humble.

Rig Veda

259

Never look down on anybody unless you're helping
them up.

Jesse Jackson

260

Blessed are they who see
beautiful things in humble
places where other people see
nothing.

Camille Pissarro

261

Humility will open more doors than arrogance ever will.

Zig Ziglar

262

For a man who walks in the light, to stay humble is not
to walk in the dark; you don't need to project yourself to
be thought an honest man.

Mike Norton

263

If I only had a little humility, I'd be perfect.

Ted Turner

264

A humble man will always receive the best that others
have to offer; for he recognizes the truth.

Jeremy Aldana

265

The only wisdom we can hope to acquire is the wisdom
of humility.

T.S. Eliot

266

Humility is not thinking less of
yourself, it's thinking of yourself
less.

C. S. Lewis

267

Self-praise is for losers. Be a
winner. Stand for something.
Always have class, and be humble.

John Madden

268

I speak to everyone in the same
way, whether he is the garbage
man or the president of the
university.

Albert Einstein

269

He who is humble is confident and wise. He who brags
is insecure and lacking.

Lisa Edmondson

Whoever loves becomes humble.
Those who love have , so to speak ,
pawned a part of their narcissism.

Sigmund Freud

271

When I look at a person, I see a person – not a rank, not
a class, not a title.

Criss Jami

272

Religion is to do right. It is to love, it is to serve, it is to
think, it is to be humble.

Ralph Waldo Emerson

273

Someone who brags is a red flag.

Maxime Lagacé

274

Success is not a good teacher, failure makes you humble.

Shahrukh Khan

275

A great man is always willing to be little.

Ralph Waldo Emerson

276

Success is a lousy teacher. It seduces smart people into thinking they can't lose.

Bill Gates

277

Pride makes us artificial and humility makes us real.

Thomas Merton

278

Humility is the solid foundation of all virtues.

Confucius

279

Think lightly of yourself and deeply of the world.

Miyamoto Musashi

280

If you're not humble, life will visit humbleness upon
you.

Mike Tyson

281

Mastery begins with humility.

Robin Sharma

282

Stars shine so they can see the world, not so the world
can see them.

Matshona Dhliwayo

283

I'm always asked, 'What's the secret to success?' But there are no secrets. Be humble. Be hungry. And always be the hardest worker in the room.

Dwayne Johnson

Dream Big

284

Dreams come in a size too big so that we may grow into them.

Josie Bisse

285

Dream no small dreams for they have no power to move the hearts of men.

Johann Wolfgang von Goethe

286

All our dreams can come true, if we have the courage to pursue them.

Walt Disney

287

At first, dreams seem impossible, then improbable, and eventually inevitable.

Christopher Reeve

288

Dying seems less sad than having lived too little.

Gloria Steinem

289

Climb high, climb far. Your goal the sky. Your aim the star.

Williams College

290

Dream as if you'll live forever... live as if you'll die today.

James Dean

291

If you don't build your dream,
someone will hire you to help build
theirs.

Tony Gaskins

292

In our dreams lies our unfinished work for the world.

Joan Chittister

293

It is not the mountain we conquer but ourselves.

Edmund Hillary

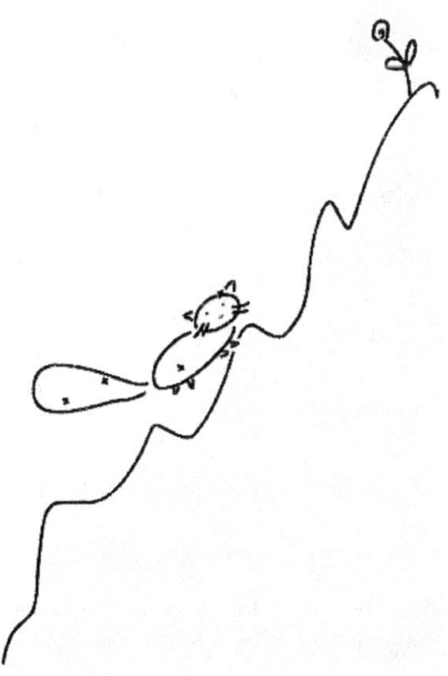

294

It's kind of fun to do the impossible!

Walt Disney

295

Let's go invent tomorrow instead of worrying about what happened yesterday.

Steve Jobs

296

Never give up on a dream just because of the time it will take to accomplish it. The time will pass anyway.

Earl Nightingale

297

Often, what seems an impossible climb is just a staircase without the steps drawn in.

Robert Brault

298

People too weak to follow their own dreams will always
find a way to discourage yours.

Bob Mayer

299

Shoot for the moon. Even if you
miss, you'll land among the
stars.

Les Brown

300

The biggest adventure you can take is to live the life of
your dreams.

Oprah Winfrey

301

The future you see is the future you get.

Robert G Allen

302

There is no straight line to a
dream.

Jack Welch

303

Whether you think you can or think you can't, you are
right.

Henry Ford

304

The future belongs to those who
believe in the beauty of their
dreams.

Eleanor Roosevelt

305

Dream big dreams; only big dreams have the power to
move men's souls.

Marcus Aurelius

306

We've removed the ceiling above our dreams. There are
no more impossible dreams.

Jesse Jackson

307

Dreams grow if you grow.

Zig Ziglar

308

If it doesn't scare you, you're probably not dreaming big
enough.

Tory Burch

309

When you have a dream you've got to grab it and never
let go.

Carol Burnett

310

Only those who dare to fail greatly can ever achieve
greatly.

Robert F. Kennedy

311

Our goals can only be reached through a vehicle of a
plan, in which we must fervently believe, and upon
which we must vigorously act. There is no other route
to success.

Pablo Picasso

312

One way to keep momentum
going is to have constantly
greater goals.

Michael Korda

Love Nature

313

There is nothing capricious in
nature and the implanting of a
desire indicates that its
gratification is in the constitution
of the creature that feels it.

Ralph Waldo Emerson

314

Nature and wisdom never are at strife.

Plutarch

315

Adopt the pace of nature; her secret is patience.

Ralph Waldo Emerson

316

Nature knows no pause in progress and development,
and attaches her curse on all inaction.

Johann Wolfgang von Goethe

317

All works are being done by the energy and power of
nature, but due to delusion of ego people assume
themselves to be the doer.

Bhagavad Gita

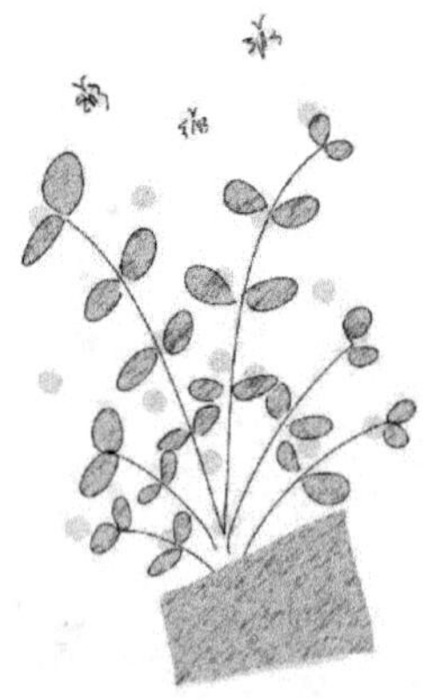

318

Nature does not hurry, yet
everything is accomplished.

Lao Tzu

319

Ever felt an angel's breath in the gentle breeze?.. A
teardrop in the falling rain? Hear a whisper amongst the
rustle of leaves? Or been kissed by a lone snowflake?
Nature is an angel's favorite hiding place.

Carrie Latet

320

Look deep into nature, and then you
will understand everything better.

Albert Einstein

321

Nature thrives on patience; man on impatience.

Paul Boese

322

One touch of nature makes the
whole world kinder.

William Shakespeare

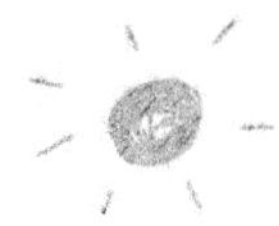

323

If you truly love nature, you will find beauty
everywhere.

Vincent Van Gogh

324

We inter-breathe with the rain forests, we drink from
the oceans. They are part of our own body.

Thich Nhat Hanh

325

In all things of nature there is something of the
marvellous.

Aristotle

326

Come forth into the light of things, let nature be your
teacher.

William Wordsworth

327

The whole secret of the study of nature lies in learning
how to use one's eyes.

George Sand

328

Choose only one master—nature.

Rembrandt

329

Preserve and
cherish the pale
blue dot, the only
home we've ever
known.

Carl Sagan

330

In nature, nothing is perfect and everything is perfect.
Trees can be contorted, bent in weird ways, and they're
still beautiful.

Alice Walker

331

Live in each season as it passes; breathe the air, drink
the drink, taste the fruit, and resign yourself to the
influence of the earth.

Henry David Thoreau

Spring is nature's way of saying, 'Let's party!'

Robin Williams

On earth there is no heaven, but there are pieces of it.

Jules Renard

334

There are always flowers for
those who want to see them.

Henri Matisse

335

...and then, I have nature and art and poetry, and if that
is not enough, what is enough?

Vincent van Gogh

336

The goal of life is to make your heartbeat match the beat
of the universe, to match your nature with Nature.

Joseph Campbell

337

Nature is not a place to visit. It is home.

Gary Snyder

Laugh out loud

338

Opportunity is missed by most people because it is
dressed in overalls and looks like work.

Thomas Eddison

339

You can't have
everything. Where would
you put it?

Steven Wright

340

A day without sunshine is
like, you know, night.

Steve Martin

341

Do not take life too seriously. You will never get out of it
alive.

Elbert Hubbard

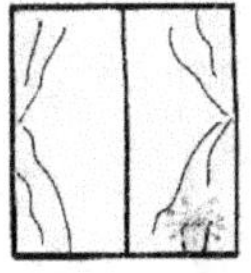

342

People say nothing is impossible, but I do nothing every day.

A.A. Milne

343

Even if you are on the right track, you'll get run over if you just sit there.

Will Rogers

344

Never put off until tomorrow
what you can do the day after
tomorrow.

Mark Twain

345

Follow your passion, stay true
to yourself, never follow
someone else's path unless
you're in the woods and you're
lost and you see a path then by
all means you should follow that.

Ellen Degeneres

346

Listen, smile, agree, and then do
whatever you were gonna do anyway.

Robert Downey Jr.

347

Never let your sense of morals prevent you from doing
what is right.

Isaac Asimov

348

A woman is like a tea bag – you can't tell how strong she
is until you put her in hot water.

Eleanor Roosevelt

349

People often say that motivation doesn't last. Well,
neither does bathing – that's why we recommend it
daily.

Zig Ziglar

350

Women who seek to be equal
with men lack ambition.

Marilyn Monroe

351

I always wanted to be somebody, but now I realize I
should have been more specific.

Lily Tomlin

352

Remember, today is the tomorrow you worried about
yesterday.

Dale Carnegie

353

I'm bored' is a useless
thing to say. I mean, you
live in a great, big, vast
world that you've seen
none percent of. Even the
inside of your own mind
is endless; it goes on
forever, inwardly, do you
understand? The fact that
you're alive is amazing,
so you don't get to say
'I'm bored.

Louis C.K.

354

If at first you don't succeed, then skydiving definitely
isn't for you.

Steven Wright

355

Here is a test to find
whether your mission on
earth is finished: If you're
alive it isn't.

Richard Bach

356

The difference between genius and stupidity is; genius
has its limits.

Albert Einstein

357

Whoever said, 'It's not whether you win or lose that
counts,' probably lost.

Martina Navratilova

358

I intend to live forever. So far, so good.

Steven Wright

I know worrying works, because none of the stuff I worried about ever happened.

Will Rogers

360

Always remember that you are absolutely unique. Just like everyone else.

Margaret Mead

361

I am an optimist. It does not seem too much use being anything else.

Winston Churchill

362

The road to success is dotted with many tempting
parking spaces.

Will Rogers

363

Be happy, it
drives people
crazy.

Lisa Lieberman-
Wang

364

The elevator to success is out of order. You'll have to
use the stairs...one step at a time.

Joe Girard

365

Tell the negative committee that meets inside your head
to sit down and shut up.

Ann Bradford

366 Bonus Quote (for a leap year)

When I hear somebody sigh, Life is hard, I am always
tempted to ask, Compared to what?

Sydney Harris

367 Bonus Quote (for good luck)

When I'm sad, I stop being sad and be awesome instead.

Barney Stinson

References